LET'S EXPLORE THE STATES

Northwest

Idaho
Oregon
Washington

John Ziff

Mason Crest
450 Parkway Drive, Suite D
Broomall, PA 19008
www.masoncrest.com

©2016 by Mason Crest, an imprint of National Highlights, Inc.

Printed and bound in the United States of America.

CPSIA Compliance Information: Batch #LES2015.
For further information, contact Mason Crest at 1-866-MCP-Book.

First printing
1 3 5 7 9 8 6 4 2

Library of Congress Cataloging-in-Publication Data

   Ziff, John.
  Northwest : Idaho, Oregon, Washington / John Ziff.
     pages cm. — (Let's explore the states)
  Includes bibliographical references and index.
  ISBN 978-1-4222-3331-3 (hc)
  ISBN 978-1-4222-8616-6 (ebook)
  1. Northwestern States—Juvenile literature. 2. Idaho—Juvenile literature.
  3. Oregon—Juvenile literature. 4. Washington (State)—Juvenile literature. I. Title.
  F597.Z54 2015
  979—dc23
                         2014050186

Let's Explore the States series ISBN: 978-1-4222-3319-1

Publisher's Note: Websites listed in this book were active at the time of publication. The publisher is not responsible for websites that have changed their address or discontinued operation since the date of publication. The publisher reviews and updates the websites each time the book is reprinted.

About the Author: Writer and editor John Ziff lives near Philadelphia.

Table of Contents

KEY ICONS TO LOOK FOR:

 Words to Understand: These words with their easy-to-understand definitions will increase the reader's understanding of the text, while building vocabulary skills.

 Sidebars: This boxed material within the main text allows readers to build knowledge, gain insights, explore possibilities, and broaden their perspectives by weaving together additional information to provide realistic and holistic perspectives.

 Research Projects: Readers are pointed toward areas of further inquiry connected to each chapter. Suggestions are provided for projects that encourage deeper research and analysis.

 Text-Dependent Questions: These questions send the reader back to the text for more careful attention to the evidence presented there.

 Series Glossary of Key Terms: This back-of-the book glossary contains terminology used throughout this series. Words found here increase the reader's ability to read and comprehend higher-level books and articles in this field.

LET'S EXPLORE THE STATES

Atlantic: North Carolina, Virginia, West Virginia

Central Mississippi River Basin: Arkansas, Iowa, Missouri

East South-Central States: Kentucky, Tennessee

Eastern Great Lakes: Indiana, Michigan, Ohio

Gulf States: Alabama, Louisiana, Mississippi

Lower Atlantic: Florida, Georgia, South Carolina

Lower Plains: Kansas, Nebraska

Mid-Atlantic: Delaware, District of Columbia, Maryland

Non-Continental: Alaska, Hawaii

Northern New England: Maine, New Hampshire, Vermont

Northeast: New Jersey, New York, Pennsylvania

Northwest: Idaho, Oregon, Washington

Rocky Mountain: Colorado, Utah, Wyoming

Southern New England: Connecticut, Massachusetts, Rhode Island

Southwest: New Mexico, Oklahoma, Texas

U.S. Territories and Possessions

Upper Plains: Montana, North Dakota, South Dakota

West: Arizona, California, Nevada

Western Great Lakes: Illinois, Minnesota, Wisconsin

Idaho
at a Glance

Area: 83,569 sq mi (216,443 sq km).
  14th largest state[1]
  Land: 82,643 sq mi (214,044 sq km)
  Water: 926 sq mi (2,398 sq km)
Highest elevation: Borah Peak,
  12,662 feet (3,859 m)
Lowest elevation: Snake River in Nez
  Perce County, 710 feet (216 m)

Statehood: July 3, 1890 (43rd state)
Capital: Boise

Population: 1,634,464
  (39th largest state)[2]

State nickname: the Gem State
State bird: mountain bluebird
State flower: syringa

[1] *U.S. Geological Survey*
[2] *U.S. Census Bureau, 2014 estimate*

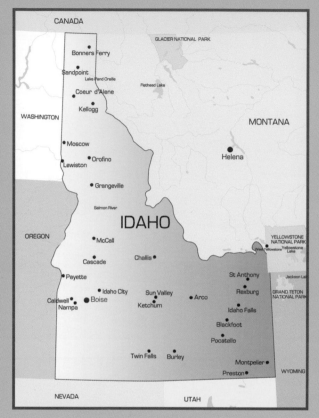

Idaho

Idaho, as many people are aware, is the nation's leading producer of potatoes. In a typical year, Idaho farmers will harvest more than 12 billion pounds of the tuberous vegetable. An amazing variety of potatoes are grown in Idaho. There's the Yukon Gold and the Yellow Finn, the Ruby Crescent and the Ida Rose, the Premier Russet, the Ranger Russet, the Clearwater Russet, and many more.

Idaho yields something else in astonishing variety: **gemstones**. Seventy-two types of precious and semiprecious stones are found in Idaho. That's the basis for Idaho's nickname, the Gem State. It's also a reflection of Idaho's diverse **geology**.

Geography

Located in the northwestern United States, Idaho borders the Canadian province of British Columbia to the north. On the east, Idaho is bounded by Montana and Wyoming. Utah and Nevada lie to the south. Oregon and Washington form Idaho's western border.

At a little more than 83,500 square miles (216,443 sq km), Idaho ranks as the 14th largest state by total area. Public lands make up 63 percent of Idaho. The federal government manages these lands, much of which are heavily forested.

Idaho's terrain is very rugged. Mountain ranges belonging to the Rocky Mountain chain extend from northern Idaho's *panhandle* into the central part of the state. These mountain ranges include the Bitterroot, Salmon River, Sawtooth, and Seven Devils. Dozens of peaks top 10,000 feet (3,000 m). Borah Peak—or Mount Borah, as Idahoans usually call it—is the highest. Located in central Idaho's Custer County, it rises to 12,662 feet (3,859 m) in the Lost River Range.

Between the mountains are a variety of valleys, gorges, and fast-moving rivers and streams. Hells Canyon, which runs along Idaho's western border with Washington and Oregon, is the deepest river gorge in North America. The Seven Devils Mountains

 # Words to Understand in This Chapter

archaeological—relating to archaeology, the scientific study of the material remains of past human cultures.

butte—an isolated hill or mountain with steep sides and a small, relatively level top.

gemstone—a mineral that, when cut and polished, can be used for jewelry.

geology—the rocks, land, and processes of land formation in a particular area.

hydroelectric—relating to the production of electricity by means of waterpower.

latitude—distance north or south of the equator, measured in degrees (up to 90 degrees).

panhandle—a narrow strip of land extending from a larger territory.

plateau—a large, relatively flat area of land that rises sharply above adjoining land on at least one side.

tributary—a stream or river that feeds a larger river or lake.

Shoshone Falls, a waterfall on the Snake River in southern Idaho, is sometimes called the "Niagara of the West." At 212 feet (65 m) high, the falls are actually 45 feet (14 m) higher than Niagara Falls.

Peaks of the Sawtooth Mountain range, near the tiny village of Stanley.

Craters of the Moon National Monument in southeastern Idaho presents a rocky landscape of lava flows, cinder cones, and sagebrush. The unusual terrain was formed by eight volcanic eruptions between 15,000 and 2,000 years ago. Today, the Craters of the Moon lava field covers 618 square miles (1,600 square km).

Rafters set out on a trip through the Snake River Canyon near Twin Falls. The canyon is 50 miles (81 km) long, with walls rising as high as 500 feet (150 meters).

rise almost a mile and a half above the surface of the Snake River at the canyon's floor.

In parts of northwest Idaho, the mountains give way to rolling hills or prairie land. But in southern Idaho, the Snake River Plain forms a dramatic break in the Rockies. This crescent-shaped depression sweeps east to west across the state for a distance of some 350 miles (563 km). Its width varies from about 30 miles to about 75 miles (48 km to 121 km). The Snake River Plain is home to most of Idaho's good farmland as well as to many of its towns and cities. Overall, it's fairly level. However, its geology is complex, and the region contains many unusual and dramatic features. These include lava fields, hot springs, *buttes*, the majestic Shoshone Falls, and even high desert sand dunes.

Mountains and valleys cover southeastern Idaho, south of the Snake River Plain. The southwestern part of the state consists largely of low mountains and *plateaus*.

Idaho has an abundance of rivers and creeks. The Snake River, which

 Did You Know?

A wildfire believed to be the largest in U.S. history ravaged the Idaho Panhandle, along with western Montana, on August 20 and 21, 1910. The Big Blowup, as the inferno came to be called, consumed about 3 million acres of forested land and claimed at least 85 lives.

runs more than 1,000 miles (1,600 km), is the most important. Originating in northwestern Wyoming, the Snake crosses into Idaho at the Palisades Reservoir in Bonneville County. The river arcs west across the Snake River Plain, enters Oregon, and then loops back, flowing northward along the Idaho-Oregon border for about 215 miles (346 km). It follows Idaho's border with Washington for another 30 miles (48 km) or so before turning west again. The Snake empties into the Columbia River in Washington. Over its entire course, the Snake drops a total of 9,500 feet (2,895 m) in elevation. This makes it highly suitable for *hydroelectric* dams, of which there are more than a dozen on the Snake. The Snake is also vital for irrigating Idaho's farms.

Other major rivers in Idaho include the Boise, Clearwater, Salmon, and Payette. All of them are *tributaries* of the Snake River.

Covering 148 square miles (383 sq km), Lake Pend Oreille (pronounced *pond oh-RAY*) is Idaho's largest lake. It's located in the northern part of the Idaho Panhandle, mostly in Bonner County but with a small portion in Kootenai County. Kootenai County

Lake Coeur d'Alene is a popular tourist spot in the Idaho Panhandle. The lake has over 109 miles (175 km) of shoreline.

also contains Coeur d'Alene (pronounced *cur duh-LANE*) Lake, which covers 50 square miles (130 sq km). Bear Lake straddles the Idaho-Utah border. The lake is 110 square miles (285 sq km), and about half of its surface area is located in southeastern Idaho's Bear Lake County.

Idaho experiences four distinct seasons. Beyond that, the climate varies considerably by region. The southern part of the state is quite dry. For example, average annual precipitation in Pocatello, located in the southeast, is only about 12 inches (31 cm). Boise, in the southwest, receives roughly the same amount. By contrast, Coeur d'Alene, in the north, averages nearly 26 inches (66 cm) of precipitation per year. Snowfall, not surprisingly, is higher in mountainous areas than in the Snake River Plain. Winter temperatures also tend to be colder at higher elevations. For instance, the average daily low in January is 10° Fahrenheit (–12° Celsius) in Idaho Falls (elevation: 4,730 feet/1,442 m), but 27°F (–3°C) in Lewiston (elevation: 1,440 feet/439

 Did You Know?

Lewiston is Idaho's only port. It's located in Nez Perce County, in the Idaho Panhandle region. Cargo loaded in Lewiston can reach the Pacific Ocean by means of the 465-mile (748-km) Columbia-Snake River System.

m). Summers tend to be hottest in the southwest. On a typical day in July, thermometers will hit 90°F (32°C) in Boise, 88°F (31°C) in Pocatello, and 85°F (29°C) in Coeur d'Alene. Humidity, however, is generally low throughout the state.

History

Native people lived on land that now makes up Idaho for thousands of years before the arrival of Europeans. Wilson Butte Cave, near Twin Falls on the Snake River Plain, is one of the earliest known *archaeological* sites within U.S. borders. Humans occupied the cave from at least 8000 BCE. And some archaeologists believe people first arrived at the site around

A Nez Perce man maneuvers a dugout canoe to the banks of a river in Idaho, circa 1900. The Nez Perce were one of several tribes that lived in this region before the arrival of Europeans in the 19th century.

13,000 BCE. Nearby caves, while not fully excavated, point to a similarly long human presence in the region.

By 1800 CE, various Indian peoples lived in the area of present-day Idaho. They included the Shoshone, Bannock, Nez Perce, Coeur d'Alene, and Kalispel.

In 1803, the United States bought from France a huge piece of territory in the center of North America. Called the Louisiana Purchase, it more than doubled the size of the country. Idaho lay just west of the Louisiana Purchase territory. Still, it was crossed in 1805 by an American expedition charged with exploring the Louisiana Purchase territory and finding a land route to the Pacific Ocean. The Lewis and Clark expedition—also known as the Corps of Discovery—entered Idaho through the Lemhi Pass, in present-day Lemhi County. The explorers eventually managed to cross Idaho's Bitterroot Mountains on their way to the Pacific coast.

The United States claimed the Pacific Northwest region. The Oregon

Country, as Americans called the territory, included all of present-day Idaho, Washington, and Oregon, along with parts of Wyoming and Montana. But the United Kingdom, Spain, and Russia also laid claim to parts of this region.

In 1809, the British established a fur-trading post at Lake Pend Oreille. An American trading post was built the following year in eastern Idaho, in present-day Fremont County.

In 1818, the United States and Britain signed a treaty that settled, at least temporarily, their dispute over the Oregon Country. The Anglo-American Convention of 1818 provided for "joint occupancy" of the Oregon Country. British and American citizens alike were permitted to settle in the territory. Spain and Russia had given up their claims to the Oregon Country by the mid-1820s.

For several decades thereafter, Idaho was a destination for very few whites beyond fur trappers and missionaries trying to convert Indians to Christianity. But from the 1840s on,

Beaver dam on an Idaho pond. In the early 19th century, British and American trappers traveled to Idaho seeking furs that could be sold for high prices in the eastern United States and Europe. Beaver fur was particularly prized.

large numbers of emigrants passed through Idaho on their way further west. Two popular routes, the Oregon Trail and the California Trail, crossed Idaho.

In 1846, Britain the United States concluded the Oregon Treaty. It ended the "joint occupancy" of the Oregon Country. By the terms of the treaty, land south of the 49th parallel of *latitude* (with the exception of Vancouver Island) belonged to the United States.

Oregon Territory—including all of present-day Oregon, Washington, and Idaho—was organized in 1848. Five years later, Washington Territory was split off, and the Idaho Panhandle became part of it. Southern Idaho remained in Oregon Territory. In 1859, when Oregon gained statehood, all of Idaho was incorporated into Washington Territory.

Gold was discovered on the Clearwater River in 1860. The following year, more gold was found on the Salmon River. News of the finds touched off a gold rush. Thousands of miners and other settlers flocked to Idaho. The growing population spurred Congress to create Idaho Territory in 1863. It initially included all of present-day Montana and nearly

Five miners in the Last Chance lead mine, in the Coeur d'Alene region of Idaho, 1910. Although gold brought the first settlers to Idaho in the 1860s, the discovery of other minerals such as silver, lead, zinc, and phosphates led to a successful mining industry. Today, more silver is mined in Idaho than in any other state.

all of Wyoming. But Idaho Territory ceded most of those lands to other territories in 1864.

Over the course of the 1800s, relations between Indians and whites in Idaho had often been strained. Localized violence was fairly common. But as increasing numbers of whites encroached on Indian lands, large-scale conflicts erupted. In January 1863, a U.S. Army cavalry unit killed nearly 250 Shoshone along the Bear River in southern Idaho. In 1877, the Nez Perce War was fought, with battlefields in Idaho, Wyoming, and Montana. U.S. Army troops fought Bannock warriors in 1878, and Shoshone in 1879. In all these conflicts, the U.S. forces eventually prevailed.

By the late 1870s, Idaho's established gold mines appeared to be largely played out. Settlement slowed. But then, in 1880, significant deposits of gold were found on the Coeur d'Alene River. Four years later, huge amounts of silver were discovered in the same region. Settlers again flooded into Idaho.

In 2010, two underground wings were built beneath the Idaho State Capitol in Boise. The building houses legislative chambers, as well as the office of Idaho's governor.

The population of Idaho Territory exceeded 88,000 by 1890. On July 3 of that year, Idaho became the 43rd state. Boise served as its capital city.

By 1900, Idaho had more than 161,000 residents. The state's population grew steadily throughout the 20th century. It surpassed half a million by 1940 and one million by 1990.

Government

Idaho has a bicameral (two-chamber) legislature. The upper chamber, the Senate, has 35 members—one from each of Idaho's 35 legislative districts. The lower chamber, the Idaho House of Representatives, has two members from each legislative district, for a total of 70 members. Senators and representatives are both elected to two-year terms, and there are no limits on the number of terms the same person may serve.

Idahoans elect their governor every

Some Famous Idahoans

Gutzon Borglum (1867–1941) is best known for carving the heads of four U.S. presidents into the granite face of Mount Rushmore in South Dakota. The sculptor was born in St. Charles, Idaho Territory.

Poet and literary critic Ezra Pound (1885–1972) was born in Hailey.

Ezra Taft Benson (1899–1994), a native of Whitney, served as president of the Church of Jesus Christ of Latter-day Saints. He was also a U.S. secretary of agriculture.

Gutzon Borglum

Born in the Idaho mining town of Wallace, Lana Turner (1921–1995) went on to become a Hollywood legend. The actress starred in more than 50 films.

In a 16-year career with Major League Baseball's Pittsburgh Pirates, pitcher Vern Law (b. 1930), the pride of Meridian, garnered 162 victories and a Cy Young Award.

Baseball Hall of Famer Harmon Killebrew (1936–2011), who blasted 574 home runs in the major leagues, learned the game in Payette.

Boise native Frank Church (1924–1984), a five-term U.S. senator, is remembered for chairing a Senate committee that investigated abuses by the U.S. intelligence agencies.

Skier Picabo Street (b. 1971) won a gold medal at the 1998 Winter Olympics. She hails, appropriately, from Triumph, Idaho.

Picabo Street

A pivot sprinkler is used to irrigate a field of potatoes on an Idaho farm. The state produces close to $1 billion worth of potatoes each year.

four years. Again, no term limits apply to the office of governor.

A small state, Idaho sends only two members to the U.S. House of Representatives. Idaho voters tend to be conservative. As of 2015, both of Idaho's congressmen, as well as its two U.S. senators, were Republicans. And no Democrat had been elected Idaho governor for 20 years.

The Economy

Farms cover more than 20 percent of Idaho's land, and agriculture is a mainstay of the state's economy. Idaho ranks number one among the states in

Night falls over Boise, the state capital and largest city.

the production of potatoes, winter peas, and lentils. It's a major producer of sugar beets, wheat, and barley. Cattle, sheep, and dairy products are other significant contributors to Idaho's agricultural sector.

Gold once lured swarms of migrants to Idaho Territory. Today, mining remains an important industry in Idaho. In 2011, according to the U.S. Geological Survey, Idaho pro-duced nearly $1.3 billion in nonfuel minerals—more than all but 16 other states. Molybdenum, phosphate rock, silver, and lead are among the most valuable products of Idaho's mining industry.

Idaho's forests, which cover more than 40 percent of the state's land, are an important resource. In 2011, Idaho ranked as the country's eighth largest lumber-producing state. Wood and paper products from Idaho generate close to $2 billion in annual sales. Other products manufactured in Idaho include electronic equipment, fabricated metal, and chemicals.

Directly or indirectly, the tourism industry supports about 7 percent of Idaho's workforce. Visitors contribute an estimated $3 billion each year to Idaho's economy.

The People

In the 1870s and 1880s, before Idaho had gained statehood, people in the Panhandle region campaigned to join Washington Territory. They believed they had more in common with residents of the Pacific Northwest than with residents of southern Idaho. To a certain extent, that attitude persists. Some people who live in northern Idaho complain that the more populous—and politically dominant—south fails to understand, or take into account, their concerns. As recently as the 1980s, local governments in the Panhandle passed resolutions calling for secession (withdrawal) from Idaho. An independent candidate for governor even made secession the cornerstone of his campaign. In spite of their differences, though, Idahoans tend to be united in the fierce pride they express for their state.

According to the U.S. Census Bureau, more than 1.6 million people live in Idaho, making the Gem State the nation's 39th largest by population. During the 1800s, Idaho was settled primarily by Americans of English, Irish, and German extraction, and by members of the Mormon faith. Today, the state remains much less racially diverse than the country overall. According to the U.S. Census Bureau, nearly 94 percent of Idaho's people are white, compared with about 78 percent nationwide. African Americans make up slightly more than 13 percent of the country's population, but just 0.8 percent of Idaho's. Idaho also has significantly lower proportions of Hispanics and Asian Americans than the United States as a whole. But a greater percentage of Native Americans live in Idaho than in the country overall (1.7 percent versus 1.2 percent).

Major Cities

With more than 212,000 residents, *Boise* is by far the largest city in Idaho. It's also the state capital and the county seat of Ada County. Boise boasts a thriving cultural scene and is home to Boise State University, which has more than 20,000 students. The city is located in southwestern Idaho, some 40 miles (64 km) from the border with Oregon.

The 2010 census counted 81,557 people in *Nampa*. Founded in the 1880s, it grew as a railroad hub. Nampa is in Canyon County, about 20 miles (32 km) west of Boise.

About 80,000 people call *Meridian* home. It's Idaho's fastest-growing city. According to the Census Bureau, Meridian's population increased by 7 percent between 2010 and 2012. Meridian is located in Ada County, about nine miles (14 km) west of Boise.

Further Reading

Stanley, John. *Idaho: Past and Present*. New York: Rosen Publishing Group, 2010.

Stapilus, Randy, and Martin Peterson. *Idaho 100: The People Who Most Influenced the Gem State*. Carlton, OR: Ridenbaugh Press, 2012.

Stefoff, Rebecca. *Idaho*. Tarrytown, NY: Marshall Cavendish Benchmark, 2008.

Internet Resources

http://history.idaho.gov/history_timeline

The Idaho State Historical Society offers a highly detailed timeline, with photos.

http://www.usgs.gov/state/state.asp?State=ID

The United States Geological Survey's "Science in Your Backyard" Web page for Idaho includes a relief map, state facts, and links to pages on subjects such as minerals, water resources, and earthquakes.

http://www.nps.gov/state/id/index.htm?program=parks

The National Park Service's page for Idaho.

 # Text-Dependent Questions

1. What are the Yukon Gold, Ruby Crescent, and Ida Rose?
2. The population of Idaho Territory spiked in the early 1860s following the discovery of what on the Clearwater and Salmon rivers?
3. What is Idaho's largest city?

 # Research Project

In 1877, the U.S. Army fought a band of heavily outnumbered Nez Perce in a conflict the *New York Times* condemned as "nothing short of a gigantic blunder and a crime." Find out how the Nez Perce War started. Trace the route of the Indians' 1,100-mile (1,770-km) fighting retreat. Where were the major battles fought? How did the war end, and what became of the Nez Perce afterward?

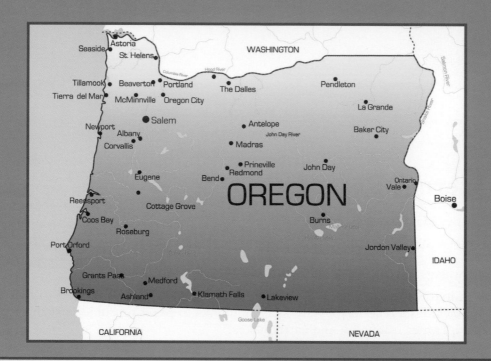

 Oregon at a Glance

Area: 98,379 sq mi (254,800 sq km)[1].
   Ninth largest state
   Land: 95,988 sq mi (248,608 sq km)
   Water: 2,391 sq mi (6,193 sq km)
Highest elevation: Mount Hood,
   11,239 feet (3,426 m)
Lowest elevation: Pacific Ocean, sea
   level

Statehood: Feb. 14, 1859 (33rd state)
Capital: Salem

Pop.: 3,970,239 (27th largest state)[2]

State nickname: the Beaver State
State bird: western meadowlark
State flower: Oregon grape

[1] U.S. Geological Survey
[2] U.S. Census Bureau, 2014 estimate

Oregon

Imagine a state where you could watch the sun rise over a desolate, windswept high desert and hike through a lush rain forest on the same day. That state is Oregon. It's a place of remarkable geographic diversity.

Geography

Oregon is located in the northwestern United States, along the Pacific coast. It has borders with four other states. Washington is to the north. Idaho lies to the east. Nevada and California form Oregon's southern boundary. On the west, Oregon is bounded by the Pacific Ocean. Its Pacific coastline is nearly 300 miles (483 km) long.

Oregon is the ninth largest state in total area. It covers more than 98,000 square miles (250,000 square kilometers).

High desert dominates the southeastern quarter of the state. This vast area—about 24,000 square miles (62,000 sq km) in all—has an average elevation of approximately 4,000 feet (1,219 m). It's a rugged region of mountains and canyons, salt lakes and salt flats, sand dunes and steep **bluffs**. But, technically speaking, most of Oregon's high desert isn't actually desert. Rather, it's **semiarid** scrubland. Typically, a true desert receives less than 10 inches (25 cm) of precipitation per year. By contrast, much of Oregon's high desert gets 12 to 15 inches (31 to 38 cm). That's enough to support vegetation such as sagebrush, hardy grasses, and even scattered juniper trees. Still, the high desert is a pretty inhospitable place. It's populated by less than one person per square mile.

Stretching across northeastern and north-central Oregon is the Columbia

Words to Understand in This Chapter

bluff—a high, steep bank.

franchise—the right to vote.

initiative—a procedure by which a specified number of voters may propose a law.

militia—a group of people who aren't part of the official armed forces of a country but who train for military service in the event of an emergency.

petition—a formal written request to a governing authority.

philanthropist—a person who donates large sums of money to make life better for other people.

prevailing winds—the winds that occur most of the time in a given area.

referendum—a public vote on a particular issue or proposed law.

semiarid—characterized by low annual rainfall (usually 10 to 20 inches).

temperate rain forest—a woodland that is located in a region with a relatively mild climate, receives a great deal of rain, is often dominated by one species of tree, and contains a large amount of moss and other vegetation growing on trees.

topography—the surface features of a particular area.

Conifer forest along the Deschutes River in central Oregon, near Redmond.

Hells Canyon is located along the border of Oregon, Washington, and Idaho. Carved by the Snake River, it is the deepest river gorge in the United States.

Plateau. The plateau extends well into Washington and also covers smaller portions of western Idaho. The Columbia Plateau was formed over millions of years as repeated volcanic eruptions deposited layer after layer of lava on the land. In Oregon the basalt—a kind of volcanic rock formed from the rapid cooling of lava—is more than a mile (1.6 km) thick in places. The *topography* of the Columbia Plateau is varied. The region contains a wide assortment of exposed basalt formations. In the northeastern corner of Oregon are two mountain ranges: the Blue Mountains and the Wallowa Mountains. Their highest peaks rise above 9,000 feet (2,700 m). On the border with Idaho, the Snake River cuts through Hells Canyon. Other rivers in the Columbia Plateau have also carved canyons. Much of the region, like the high desert, is semi-arid.

A major mountain range marks the western limit of the Columbia Plateau. The Cascades extend northward from northern California, separating the western third of Oregon from the rest of the state. The range continues through Washington and reaches into Canada.

The Cascades' highest peaks are on the eastern side of the range. Many of them are volcanoes. In Oregon, these include Mount Hood, which at 11,239 feet (3,426 m) is the state's highest elevation; a trio of peaks known as the Three Sisters, all of which are over 10,000 feet (3,000 m); Mount Jefferson (10,497 feet/3,200 m); and Mount Bachelor (9,068 feet/2,764 m). East of the high peaks are foothills and plateaus. Elevations remain above 3,000 feet (914 m), except around the Columbia River Gorge, along Oregon's border with Washington.

The western side of the Cascades is made up of mountains ranging from about 4,000 to 6,000 feet (1,200 to 1,800 m). These mountains were once much taller. But they're a lot older than the peaks on the eastern side of the Cascades and have eroded over many millions of years.

The Cascades are high enough to create a "rain shadow." The *prevailing winds* blow from the west, picking up moisture from the Pacific Ocean. But as the air is swept upward toward the top of the Cascades, it cools. This causes the moisture to condense and fall as rain or snow. The air that passes over the mountains is very dry. This explains why the western slopes of the Cascades can receive more than 100 inches (254 cm) of precipitation annually, while areas to the east of the mountains get 15 inches (38 cm) or less.

In the southwestern corner of Oregon, the Cascades give way to the Klamath Mountains. They extend to the Pacific coast. In the northern half of the state, a broad, flat basin lies west of the Cascades. The Willamette Valley contains fertile soil and is home to Oregon's most productive farmland. It's also home to the state's

A meadow on the slopes of Mount Hood, in the Cascades of western Oregon.

largest cities. The much smaller Umqua and Rogue valleys are south of the Willamette Valley.

To the west of the Willamette Valley is the Oregon Coast Range. The mountain range has three sections: northern, central, and southern. Elevations top 4,000 feet (1,200 m) in the central section but average about 1,500 feet (450 m) overall. The Coast Range contains areas of *temperate rain forest*.

Crater Lake is the deepest lake in the United States. Its sky-blue waters reach a depth of 1,943 feet (592 m). About 7,500 years ago, the cone of a volcano, Mount Mazama, collapsed after a large eruption. Over many centuries, the resulting volcanic crater—called a caldera—filled with water, creating Crater Lake.

Oregon has more than 110,000 miles (177,000 km) of rivers and streams. The most important river is the Columbia. Flowing west, it forms more than 300 miles (482 km) of Oregon's border with Washington. Hydroelectric dams on the Columbia provide power to the region. Other major rivers in Oregon include the Willamette, Deschutes, and John Day. All are major tributaries of the Columbia River. So is the Snake River, which runs along Oregon's border with Idaho.

At about 140 square miles (363 sq km), Upper Klamath Lake is Oregon's largest freshwater lake by surface area. It's located in southern Oregon's Klamath County. So, too, is scenic Crater Lake, the centerpiece of Oregon's only national park.

The Cascade Range divides Oregon's wet western region from the dry eastern part of the state. But with the exception of winter at high elevations, temperatures across Oregon tend to be moderate year-round. For example, in Eugene—located in the Willamette Valley—the average daily low temperature for January is 33°F (1°C), and the average high is 47°F (8°C). High temperatures for July, the warmest month, average 81°F (27°C). By comparison, in the high desert city of Burns, daily July high temperatures average just 86°F (30°C).

History

Spanish sailors may have sighted the coast of Oregon as early as the 1540s. But in 1579, the English sea captain Francis Drake landed in northern California or Oregon. Drake and his crew spent more than a month ashore, during which they made contact with Native Americans. Groups living in Oregon at the time included the Coquille, Chinook, Klamath, Nez Perce, Tillamook, and Umpqua. Drake claimed the region for England.

But two centuries would pass before significant European interest in the Northwest. During the second half of the 18th century, British, Spanish, and French expeditions explored the coast. In 1788–89, an English sea captain and an American sea captain both traded with Indians along the Oregon coast. The American captain, Robert Gray of Boston, returned to the area in 1792. On that voyage, Gray sailed over a treacherous sandbar and anchored in the Columbia River.

In 1805, Lewis and Clark's expedition traveled overland to reach the Pacific coast. During the last leg of their journey, the Corps of Discovery followed the Columbia River. It provided the only low-elevation route through the Cascades. The explorers built Fort Clatsop on the south side of the Columbia River, in present-day Oregon. There, they spent the winter of 1805–06. In part this was to estab-lish U.S. claims to the region.

But for decades the United States and Great Britain would dispute ownership of the Pacific Northwest. Americans called the region Oregon Country. The British referred to it as the Columbia District.

In 1811, the Pacific Fur Company established a small trading post on the southern shores of the Columbia, near the mouth of the great river. The settlement was called Fort Astoria, after John Jacob Astor, the New York–based owner of the Pacific Fur Company. Fort Astoria's manager, Duncan McDougall, sold the post to a

Reconstructed buildings at the site of Fort Clatsop, near present-day Astoria, where the Lewis and Clark expedition spent the winter of 1805–06.

Between 1840 and 1880, hundreds of thousands of American pioneers made their way west to the Oregon Territory, carrying their possessions in covered wagons pulled by oxen.

Canadian fur-trading company in 1813. The United States and Britain were fighting the War of 1812, and McDougall realized the fort couldn't be defended.

The Anglo-American Convention of 1818 gave American and British citizens equal rights in the Oregon Country. But the British weren't interested in settling the region. Rather, they wanted to ensure control of the fur trade by the British-owned Hudson's Bay Company.

During the 1840s, though, the Oregon Country became a major destination for American pioneers. A trickle of migrants in 1841 was followed, two years later, by what came to be called the Great Migration. Departing from Independence, Missouri, about 1,000 pioneers—with more than a hundred wagons and 5,000 head of cattle—made their way some 2,000 miles (3,200 km) west to the Willamette Valley. Each year for decades thereafter, thousands would undertake the long trek over the Oregon Trail.

The flood of American settlers soon convinced the British that

Haystack Rock is a well-known landmark at Cannon Beach. The rock rises 235 feet (72 m) above the ocean. Similar rock formations can be found all along the state's Pacific coast.

The Bonneville Dam is on the Columbia River at the border between Oregon and Washington. Built in the 1930s, the dam generates electrical power for several Oregon communities.

defending the interests of the Hudson's Bay Company in the Pacific Northwest was a hopeless cause. In June 1846, the United States and the United Kingdom signed the Oregon Treaty. Under the agreement, the British gave up their claims to land south of the 49th parallel of latitude.

Settlers in the Willamette Valley had set up a provisional, or temporary, government in 1843. In December 1847, the provisional legislature drafted a *petition* to the U.S. Congress. It asked for territorial status for the Oregon Country. Congress agreed. In August 1848, Oregon Territory came into being. It included present-day Idaho and Washington, as well as parts of Montana and Wyoming.

The Donation Land Claim Act gave 320 acres of free land to single men (or 640 acres to married couples) who settled in Oregon Territory before December 1850. The law, plus the discovery of gold in southwestern Oregon, spurred another big influx of newcomers. As whites pushed Indians from the land and destroyed the food sources they'd traditionally relied on

 Did You Know?

The Oregon Trail began in western Missouri and cut across Kansas, Nebraska, Wyoming, and Idaho before ending in Oregon's Willamette Valley. Between the early 1840s and the early 1880s, an estimated 500,000 pioneers made their way west on the Oregon Trail. The 2,000-mile (3,219-km) trek typically took 140 to 160 days. The Oregon Trail quickly fell out of use after the Union Pacific Railroad opened a line to the Northwest in 1884.

to survive, a series of conflicts erupted. By the late 1850s, the U.S. Army and settler *militias* had crushed the Indians, who were forced onto reservations.

On February 14, 1859, Oregon was admitted to the Union. It had shed Washington, Idaho, and the parts of Montana and Wyoming that had belonged to Oregon Territory.

At the time Oregon became the 33rd state, the nation was bitterly divided over the issue of slavery. The

Civil War would explode just two years later. Oregon's state constitution banned slavery. But it also prohibited blacks from moving into the state. Those already in Oregon were permitted to remain, though they weren't allowed to own real estate. The "exclusion clause" of Oregon's constitution wouldn't be repealed until 1926.

In the years after the Civil War, several railroad lines were constructed in Oregon. This provided a major boost for the state's farmers and timber interests. Their products became much easier to move to market. Economic growth spurred population

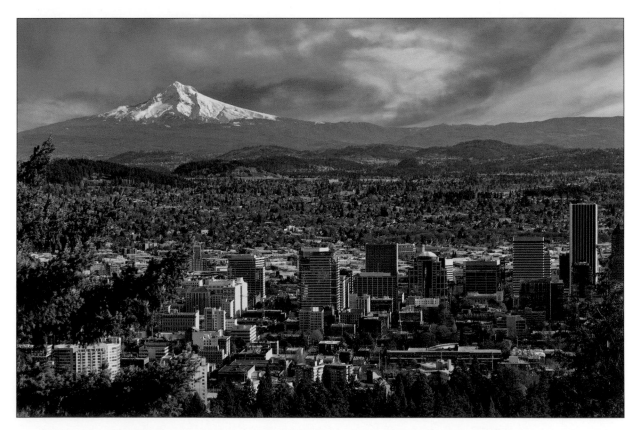

Sunrise over Portland, the state's largest city. Mount Hood looms in the background.

growth. Between 1870 and 1890, Oregon's population increased by more than 450 percent, from about 91,000 to about 413,000.

During the 1930s, the Bonneville Dam was constructed on the Columbia River, about 40 miles (64 km) east of Portland. It began supplying hydroelectric power to the region in 1938. Cheap electricity would prove key to Oregon's industrial development.

John Kitzhaber served two terms as governor of Oregon, from 1995 until 2003. He was reelected governor in 2010, and won a second term in 2014. However, in February 2015 Kitzhaber was forced to resign due to a scandal.

Government

The Oregon Legislative Assembly consists of the 30-seat Senate and the 60-seat House of Representatives. Senators are elected to four-year terms. Representatives are elected to two-year terms. Legislators aren't subject to term limits.

The Legislative Assembly is a part-time body. In odd-numbered years, it meets for no more than 160 days. In even-numbered years, legislative sessions are limited to 35 days.

Oregonians elect their governor every four years. Governors may not serve more than two terms in succes-

sion. But a two-term governor may run again after being out of office for four years.

Since 1902, Oregon's citizens have enjoyed a measure of "direct democracy." Instead of relying only on the Legislative Assembly to create laws, Oregon's voters may do so through ballot *initiatives* and referenda. If 6 percent of registered voters sign a petition, a proposed change in Oregon's legal code is placed on the ballot. Then, if a majority of voters approve the initiative, it becomes law. Oregonians can also reject, by *referendum*, any law passed by the legislature. Eight percent of registered voters must sign a petition to get a referendum on the ballot.

Some Famous Oregonians

In part because of the work of writer, editor, and women's rights advocate Abigail Scott Duniway (1834–1915), women in Oregon were able to vote eight years before the *franchise* was guaranteed to women nationwide.

Abigail Duniway

Scientist and activist Linus Pauling (1901–1994) won a Nobel Prize in Chemistry and a Nobel Peace Prize. He grew up in Portland and Condon.

Beverly Cleary (b. 1916), the author of such books as *Dear Mr. Henshaw, Ralph S. Mouse*, and *Ramona Quimby, Age 8*, has been captivating young readers since the 1950s. Cleary was raised in Yamhill and Portland.

Writer Ken Kesey (1935–2001), who spent much of his childhood and youth in Springfield, is best known for his novel *One Flew Over the Cuckoo's Nest*.

Businessman and *philanthropist* Phil Knight (b. 1938) is the chairman and cofounder of Nike. The company's other founder was legendary track and field coach William "Bill" Bowerman (1911–1999), who was born in Portland and spent 24 years as the head coach at the University of Oregon.

One of the 31 Olympic runners that Bowerman coached was Coos Bay native Steve Prefontaine (1951–1975). "Pre" set numerous American records in middle and long distance running, and his popularity led many people to take up running in the 1970s.

Portland native Matt Groening (b. 1954) created the popular animated TV series *The Simpsons*, which began airing in 1989. He also created the series *Futurama*.

Before patrolling center field for the Boston Red Sox and the New York Yankees, Jacoby Ellsbury (b. 1983) starred on his high school team in Madras and at Oregon State University.

Matt Groening

Oregon is allotted five seats in the U.S. House of Representatives, in addition to its two U.S. senators.

The Economy

Agriculture, fishing, and forest products drove Oregon's economy for much of the state's history. While those sectors aren't quite as central today, they remain significant.

Greenhouse and nursery products (such as flower bulbs) are the most valuable part of Oregon's agricultural sector. They were worth $742.5 million in 2011. Other important agricultural products included hay, cattle, and wheat.

The success of Oregon's commercial fishing industry can vary significantly from year to year. In 2012, a

A log loader fills the rear trailer of a log truck in southern Oregon.

good year, the total catch was valued at more than $170 million. Salmon, Dungeness crab, shrimp, tuna, and sardines are among the leading species caught.

Oregon leads all U.S. states in the production of plywood and softwood lumber, materials that are essential in the construction of houses. In 2012, the forest sector contributed nearly $13 billion to Oregon's economy and employed approximately 76,000 Oregonians.

In recent decades, manufacturing has assumed an increasingly important role in Oregon's economy. Among the leading manufactured products are aluminum, chemicals, electronics, and computer components.

The People

A Gallup poll conducted from June to December 2013 asked residents of all 50 states whether they'd relocate to another state if they had the chance. Nationally, one-third of the people polled said they'd move. But in Oregon, the figure was just 24 percent—lower than all other states except Hawaii, Maine, and Montana (23 percent). Clearly, Oregonians believe their state is a nice place to live.

The familiar "swoosh" symbol identifies a Nike, Inc. store in Japan. Nike is one of the world's largest manufacturers of sports apparel and athletic shoes. Founded in Oregon during the early 1970s, the company today employs more than 40,000 people around the world.

Eugene is Oregon's second-largest city.

The 2010 U.S. census counted more than 3.8 million Oregonians, making Oregon the country's 27th largest state by population. According to the Census Bureau, 88.3 percent of Oregon's people are non-Hispanic whites. That's more than 10 percent higher than the proportion of non-Hispanic whites in the nation overall. Nine decades after the repeal of Oregon's "exclusion laws," African Americans still make up only 2 percent of the state's population (compared with 13.1 percent nationwide). Oregon has a higher proportion of American Indians than the country overall (1.8 percent versus 1.2 percent).

Major Cities

With a population of more than 600,000, **Portland** is Oregon's largest city. It's located in Multnomah

The Oregon State Capitol Building is located in Salem.

tech industry. It's also considered one of the most environmentally friendly cities in the country.

Located at the southern end of the Willamette Valley, *Eugene* (2010 population: 156,185) is the county seat of Lane County. It boasts a vibrant arts scene and is known as a haven for outdoor-sports enthusiasts. Eugene is home to the University of Oregon, where more than 20,000 students are enrolled.

Oregon's capital city, *Salem*, straddles the Willamette River in the central Willamette Valley. It has more than 155,000 residents.

County, in the northern part of the Willamette Valley. The Willamette River cuts through the city shortly before emptying into the Columbia, which separates Portland from Vancouver, Washington. Portland is the center of Oregon's booming high-

The 2010 census counted more than 105,000 residents of *Gresham*. Oregon's fourth largest city is located directly east of Portland.

Further Reading

Hayes, Derek. *Historical Atlas of Washington and Oregon.* Oakland: University of California Press, 2011.

Klausmeyer, David. *Oregon Trail Stories: True Accounts of Life in a Covered Wagon.* Guilford, CT: Globe Pequot Press, 2003.

Kyi, Tanya Lloyd. *Oregon.* Vancouver, British Columbia: Whitecap Books Ltd., 2010.

Internet Resources

http://bluebook.state.or.us/

The online version of the *Oregon Blue Book*, the state's official almanac and fact book, offers a wealth of information on a wide variety of subjects.

http://www.oregonencyclopedia.org/

The Oregon Historical Society touts its *Oregon Encyclopedia* as "An Authoritative and Free Resource on All Things Oregon."

http://www.oregon.com/living/state_facts

Fun facts about Oregon.

http://www.history.com/topics/us-states/oregon

From the History.com website, this page provides facts about Oregon, as well as historic photographs of the state.

http://www.netstate.com/states/geography/or_geography.htm

This site provides detailed information about Oregon's geography.

 # Text-Dependent Questions

1. What is a rain shadow?
2. Which valley contains Oregon's largest cities?
3. What was the Anglo-American Convention of 1818?

 # Research Project

Investigate the Lewis and Clark expedition. There are many excellent books and Internet sites devoted to the subject. After consulting a few of these sources, write a one-page report about the winter the explorers spent at Fort Clatsop. What was their daily life like? What difficulties did they face?

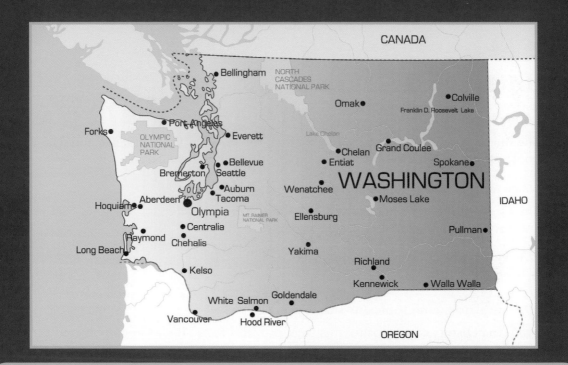

Washington at a Glance

Area: 71,298 sq mi (184,661 sq km)[1].
18th largest state
Land: 66,456 sq mi (172,120 sq km)
Water: 4,842 sq mi (12,541 sq km)
Highest elevation: Mount Rainier,
14,411 feet (4,393 m)
Lowest elevation: Pacific Ocean, sea
level

Statehood: Nov. 11, 1889 (42nd state)
Capital: Olympia

Pop.: 7,061,530 (13th largest state)[2]

State nickname: the Evergreen State
State bird: willow goldfinch
State flower: coast rhododendron

[1] *U.S. Census Bureau*
[2] *U.S. Census Bureau, 2014 estimate*

Washington

ashington is a state of stunning natural beauty. It's home to snowcapped volcanoes and crystal-clear *alpine* lakes, to towering old-growth forests and plunging river canyons, to rugged beaches, islands, and *fjords*.

Geography

Washington occupies the northwestern corner of the **contiguous United States**. It borders the Canadian province of British Columbia to the north, Idaho to the east, and Oregon to the south.

Washington ranks as the 18th largest state by total area. It covers nearly 71,300 square miles (185,000 sq km).

The Columbia Plateau dominates eastern Washington. The plateau extends—in a roughly triangular shape—from the Idaho and Oregon borders into the center of Washington. Much of the land is level or consists of rolling hills. But the Columbia and Snake rivers cut dramatic canyons through the region, and high ridges reach elevations of about 4,000 feet (1,219 m) near the western edge of the plateau. As is the case with eastern Oregon, eastern Washington is a dry region. Semiarid grasslands cover much of the Columbia Plateau.

North of the Columbia Plateau, in the northeastern part of Washington, is the Okanogan Highlands. Here, parallel mountains running in a north to south direction are separated by narrow valleys. Elevations reach 8,000 feet (2,400 m) in places.

In west-central Washington, the Okanogan Highlands and the Columbia Plateau give way to the majestic Cascade Range. Washington's Cascades include five active volcanoes: Glacier Peak, Mount Adams, Mount Baker, Mount Rainier, and Mount St. Helens. Rising 14,411 feet (4,393 m) above sea level, Mount Rainier is Washington's highest point. In Washington, as in Oregon, the Cascades create a rain shadow. Abundant precipitation—especially snow—falls on the western slopes. Dry conditions prevail on the eastern face of the range, though.

The western side of the Cascades gives way to low-lying land. Southern Washington's Clark County contains a small part of the Willamette Valley. North of that is the Puget Lowland,

Words to Understand in This Chapter

alpine—relating to or characteristic of high mountains.
contiguous United States—the United States excluding Alaska and Hawaii.
fjord—a narrow inlet of the sea between cliffs or steep slopes (pronounced *FEE-ord*).
plutonium—a heavy, unstable metallic element that that can be used in nuclear bombs.
slogan—a word or phrase, typically repeated frequently, that is used to express support for a particular position or to gain support for some goal.

Mount Rainier and Tipsoo Lake in winter.

Waves crash against the rocky coastline near Lime Kiln Lighthouse on San Juan Island, the second-largest and most populous of the islands (known collectively as the San Juan Islands) that lie off the coast of Washington.

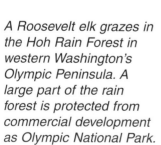

A Roosevelt elk grazes in the Hoh Rain Forest in western Washington's Olympic Peninsula. A large part of the rain forest is protected from commercial development as Olympic National Park.

which wraps around Puget Sound and stretches to the border with Canada.

Puget Sound is a deep inlet that extends southward about 100 miles (160 km) from the eastern end of the Strait of Juan de Fuca, which separates Washington's Olympic Peninsula from Canada's Vancouver Island. Puget Sound is fed saltwater by Pacific Ocean tides that enter through the Strait of Juan de Fuca, and freshwater by 11 major rivers than empty into it. It has multiple channels, fjords, and islands. It's rimmed by cities, including Seattle, Tacoma, and Olympia.

Washington's shoreline also extends north from the Strait of Juan de Fuca, to the Strait of Georgia. That body of water separates Vancouver Island from the mainland of British Columbia and Washington. At the lower end of the Strait of Georgia are the San Juan Islands. They belong to Washington.

The Olympic Peninsula is bounded on the west by the Pacific Ocean, on the north by the Strait of Juan de Fuca, and on the east by Puget Sound.

 Did You Know?

Washington—like Oregon and California—sits on the so-called Ring of Fire. The Ring of Fire is a horseshoe-shaped area of intense volcanic and earthquake activity. It stretches about 25,000 miles (40,234 km), from southern Chile up the western coasts of South and North America, across Alaska's Aleutian Island chain, down the eastern edge of Asia, eastward through New Guinea, and then south to New Zealand. The earthquakes and volcanic activity along the Ring of Fire occur where giant plates of the Earth's crust rub together or collide.

The peninsula contains the Olympic Mountains. The range's highest peak, Mount Olympus, rises nearly 8,000 feet (2,400 m). The western slopes of the Olympic Mountains feature some of the rainiest places in the United States. The Hoh Rain Forest, for example, can receive more than 14 feet of rain per year.

South of the Olympic Peninsula, Washington's Pacific coastline includes two large bays: Grays Harbor and Willapa Bay. Just inland from the latter are the Willapa Hills, which top 3,100 feet (945 m) in places. The Willapa Hills are bounded on the south by the Columbia River.

The Columbia is Washington's longest river. After entering the north-eastern part of the state from British Columbia, it flows some 740 miles (1,191 km) before emptying into the Pacific Ocean on Washington's southern border with Oregon. Other major rivers in Washington include the Snake, a tributary of the Columbia that crosses the southeastern part of

The Columbia River Gorge is a canyon along the border between Washington and Oregon. The canyon is as deep as 4,000 feet (1,200 m) in places, and runs for more than 80 miles (130 km).

Heavy rain and snow in Washington occasionally leads to catastrophic mudslides that can close roads and destroy property. One major hillside collapse in March 2014 wiped out nearly 50 homes in the small community of Oso, killing 43 people.

the state; and the Yakima, which rises in the Cascades and flows southeastward before emptying into the Columbia near the city of Richland.

Lake Chelan, located in north-central Washington's Chelan County, is the state's largest natural lake by surface area. It covers 52 square miles (135 sq km). The largest manmade lake in Washington is Franklin D. Roosevelt Lake, at 125 square miles (324 sq km). Located in the northeastern part of the state, it was created by the Grand Coulee Dam on the Columbia River.

As is the case with Oregon, the Cascades play a major role in Washington's climate. Ample precipitation falls west of the mountains, and temperatures there tend to be mild year-round. In Seattle, for example, a typical day in January features a low temperature of about 36°F (2°C) and a high of about 47°F (8°C). The average daily temperature range in July is between 56°F and 75°F (13°C and 24°C).

East of the Cascades, conditions are drier, and seasonal temperature variations are generally more dramatic. In Spokane, for example, average daily highs in January are 34°F (1°C), barely above the freezing mark. Meanwhile, July highs average about 83°F (28°C).

History

Before the arrival of whites, numerous native peoples occupied the territory that makes up today's state of Washington. Tribes that lived east of the Cascades included the Cayuse, Nez Perce, Palouse, Spokane, and Yakima. The Chinook, Lummi, Quinault, and Snohomish were among the tribes occupying coastal areas.

In 1775, the sea captain Bruno de

American sailors fight with Native Americans on the Pacific coast during Captain Robert Gray's exploration of Oregon and Washington in the early 1790s.

Heceta commanded a Spanish expedition to explore and map the Pacific coast of North America. During the expedition, Heceta landed at the site of present-day Point Grenville, Washington. He claimed the Pacific Northwest region, and territory as far north as Alaska, for Spain.

Other countries refused to recognize Spain's claims, however. Britain's Captain James Cook charted the western coast of the Olympic Peninsula in 1778. He claimed the area for the British crown. Further British exploration—and the beginnings of trade with Pacific Northwest Indians—occurred in the years that followed. In 1790, Spain avoided a possible war with Great Britain through an agreement recognizing the right of citizens of both countries to explore or trade in the Northwest.

Captain Robert Gray's 1792 push into the mouth of the Columbia River, and the arrival of Lewis and Clark in 1805, signaled U.S. interest in the region. Spain formally abandoned its claims to the Pacific Northwest in 1819, a year after the Anglo-American

Convention provided for joint British and American occupation of the Oregon Country. The Oregon Country was understood to include the present-day states of Oregon, Idaho, and Washington, but also the western coast of Canada all the way north to Alaska. At the time, Alaska was claimed by Russia.

President James K. Polk threatened war with Great Britain over the disputed Oregon country, which included the present-day state of Washington.

The British and Americans both regarded the Anglo-American Convention as a temporary measure. In the end, they believed, the two nations couldn't share territory.

Americans generally were willing to divide the Oregon Country at 49°N latitude. That would simply extend to the Pacific Ocean the existing border between British North America (Canada) and the United States.

But the British wanted territory as far south as 42°N—the southern border of the present-day state of Oregon. The British strategy, termed the fur desert policy, was to completely eliminate the beaver population from the Snake River Basin. Seeing that there were no valuable furs to be obtained, the British reasoned, Americans would be discouraged from moving farther west. This would ensure that the royally chartered Hudson's Bay Company controlled the Oregon Country. And the company could reap big profits exploiting the region's supply of furs.

But, beginning in the 1840s, large numbers of Americans moved into the Oregon Country in spite of the British fur desert policy. The Americans were settlers rather than trappers. They intended to stay on the land.

The Oregon Country became a major issue during the 1844 U.S. presidential campaign. The Democratic Party's nominee, James K. Polk, staked out a very aggressive position. He declared that all of the Oregon

Olympia became the capital city of Washington Territory in 1853. After Washington gained statehood in 1889, the present capitol building was constructed on the site where an earlier wooden structure had housed the territorial legislature. In the early 1910s, additional government buildings were constructed around the state capitol building. Today, the capitol building contains chambers where the two houses of the state legislature meet, as well as the governor's office.

Country, not just the territory south of 49°N, should belong to the United States. Polk hinted that the United States might go to war over the issue. His supporters rallied behind the *slogan* "Fifty-four Forty or Fight!"—54°40' being the latitude where the Oregon Country ended and Russian Alaska began.

Polk won the election. Soon after taking office, he informed the British that joint occupation of the Oregon Country would end in one year. Despite his campaign bluster, however, President Polk was willing to accept less than the entire Oregon Country. In 1846, the United States and the United Kingdom hammered out the Oregon Treaty. It set the boundary between the United States and British North America at 49°N. Although that line of latitude cuts across the southern part of Vancouver Island, the treaty gave the entire island to the British.

In 1848, when Oregon Territory was organized, Washington was part of it. Five years later, in 1853, Washington Territory was created. It included the Idaho Panhandle and part of western Montana. Over the following decade, the borders of Washington Territory would change several times. The current boundaries of Washington were fixed in 1863.

Washington gained statehood on November 11, 1889. It was the 42nd state admitted to the Union. At the time, Washington's population was just under 350,000. By 1900, more than a half million people were living in the state.

In 1933, construction began on a massive dam across the Columbia River in northeastern Washington. The Grand Coulee Dam began providing hydroelectric power to the region in 1942. It helped fuel Washington's industrial development.

Washington played a major role in the U.S. war effort during World War II. The Puget Sound area was a center of shipbuilding and aircraft production. The Hanford nuclear facility in south-central Washington's Benton County produced ***plutonium*** for one of the two atomic bombs the United States dropped on Japan to end the war.

But Washington, along with California and Oregon, also witnessed a tragic and shameful episode during

When the Grand Coulee Dam was completed in 1942, it was one of the tallest dams in the United States, at 550 feet (170 m). Today, this dam on the Columbia River produces more hydroelectric power than any other American facility.

The eruption of Mount St. Helens in 1980 devastated an area of more than 150 square miles (389 sq km) and killed 57 people.

World War II. In March 1942—three months after Japan's attack on Pearl Harbor, Hawaii—President Franklin D. Roosevelt signed an order under which more than 120,000 Japanese Americans living on the West Coast were rounded up and imprisoned in remote internment camps. They weren't permitted to return to their homes until January 1945.

In 1980, Washingtonians were reminded of the dangers of living near volcanoes. On May 18 of that year, Mount St. Helens exploded. The eruption killed 57 people and caused more than a billion dollars in damage.

Between 2004 and 2008, an increase in volcanic activity was observed at Mount St. Helens, but this time there was no major eruption.

Government

Washington has 49 legislative districts. Voters in each district elect one member to the Washington State Senate and two members to the Washington State House of Representatives. Senators are elected to four-year terms. Representatives serve terms of two years. Neither senators nor representatives are limited in the number of terms they may serve.

Washingtonians elect a governor every four years. No term limits apply.

Washington sends 10 members to

The aircraft manufacturer Boeing was founded in Seattle during the early 20th century. The company's airplane assembly plant in Everett is the world's largest building by volume, at 472 million cubic feet (13.4 million cubic meters).

the U.S. House of Representatives. As of 2015, Washington was one of just three states whose U.S. senators were both women.

The Economy

In Washington's economy, traditional sectors like agriculture and manufac- turing share the stage with some of the most prominent companies of the digital era. In the latter category is Microsoft, which is headquartered in Redmond. Its Windows software runs about 9 of every 10 computers world- wide. Amazon.com, based in Seattle, is the world's largest online retailer.

Some Famous Washingtonians

Bertha Knight Landes (1868–1943) was the first female mayor of a major American city. She became mayor of Seattle in 1926.

Actor and singer Bing Crosby (1903–1977) grew up in Spokane. He was one of the most successful performers in the first half of the 20th century.

Many music critics rank Jimi Hendrix (1942–1970) as the greatest rock guitarist of all time. He was born and raised in Seattle.

Seattle native Bill Gates (b. 1955), a businessman, computer programmer, inventor, and philanthropist, cofounded the software company Microsoft.

Bill Gates

Ryne Sandberg (b. 1959), a Hall of Fame second baseman, learned to play baseball in Spokane.

Writer Sherman Alexie (b. 1966) grew up on the Spokane Indian Reservation. His books, which include *Reservation Blues*, reflect the experiences of Native Americans in the Northwest.

Lifelong Washingtonian Kurt Cobain (1967–1994) fronted the legendary grunge band Nirvana.

Actress Hilary Swank (b. 1974), a two-time Academy Award winner, grew up in Spokane and Bellingham.

Goalkeeper Hope Solo (b. 1981) helped lead the United States women's national soccer team to gold medals at the 2008 and 2012 Summer Olympics. Solo hails from Richland.

Apolo Ohno (b. 1982), born and raised in Seattle, won eight Olympic medals in short-track speed skating.

Bellevue-born Tim Lincecum (b. 1984), a pitcher for the San Francisco Giants, owns two Cy Young Awards and three World Series rings.

Pro Football Hall of Fame quarterback John Elway (b. 1960) grew up in Washington.

Apolo Ohno

Hilary Swank

Bellevue is home to Expedia Inc., the world's largest online travel company.

Washington is the country's leading producer of apples. Other important fruit crops include grapes, raspberries, cherries, and pears. Washington farmers produce about three-quarters of the hops grown in the United States. Hops are a key ingredient in beer.

Items manufactured in Washington range from lumber and paper products to chemicals, aluminum, and electronics. Washington is a leader in aircraft production, thanks largely to the huge Boeing plant located in Everett.

The People

In 2013, the American Psychological Association published the results of a 12-year study examining personality traits of people in the various states. The research found that residents of Washington tend to be relaxed and creative—a finding that is in keeping with popular wisdom about Washingtonians.

According to the U.S. Census Bureau, there are more than 7 million residents of Washington, making the Evergreen State the nation's 13th largest by population.

An aerial view of Microsoft's Redmond campus, with Lake Sammamish in the background. The company was founded in 1975, and today is a worldwide leader in the production of computer operating systems and software, games, and electronic devices. Microsoft has annual sales of more than $86 billion.

The Space Needle (left) is a distinctive feature of Seattle's skyline. This landmark, built for the 1962 World's Fair, is 605 feet (184 m) high.

Interstate 90 passes through Spokane, Washington's second-largest city. I-90 is the nation's longest highway, stretching across the country from Boston to Seattle.

Washington has a slightly higher percentage of white residents than the United States overall. It also has higher proportions of Asian Americans, American Indians, and people of Native Hawaiian/Pacific Islander ancestry. According to the Census Bureau, African Americans make up 13.1 percent of the U.S. population, but just 3.9 percent of Washington residents. Similarly, while close to 17 percent of the country's residents are Latinos, in Washington the figure is only 11.7 percent.

Major Cities

With an estimated population of more than 634,000, *Seattle* is the largest city in the Pacific Northwest. It sits on a strip of land bounded on the west by Puget Sound, and on the east by Lake Washington. The sun doesn't shine much on Seattle—the city averages about 225 days of heavy cloud cover per year (the most of any major U.S. city), and the drizzle is seemingly endless. But Seattle offers plenty of business, cultural, and recreational opportunities, and surveys consistently rank it as one of the best places in the country to live.

About 209,000 people live in *Spokane*, Washington's second largest city. It's located in the eastern part of the state, about 20 miles (32 km) from the Idaho border.

Tacoma, a city of more than 200,000, boasts Washington's largest port. It's located on Puget Sound, about 30 miles (48 km) south of Seattle.

Vancouver, Washington (not to be confused with Vancouver, British Columbia), is located in Clark County, in the southwestern part of the state. It has a population of about 165,000.

The 2010 census counted 122,363 residents of *Bellevue*. A suburb of Seattle, it sits on the eastern banks of Lake Washington.

Washington's capital, *Olympia*, is located on Budd Inlet, at the far southern end of Puget Sound. More than 47,000 people call Olympia home.

Further Reading

Denny, Arthur Armstrong. *Pioneer Days on Puget Sound*. Charleston, SC: Nabu Press, 2012.

Strudwick, Leslie. *Washington*. New York: Weigl Publishers Inc., 2011.

Walker, Sally, and Douglas W. Owsley. *Their Skeletons Speak: Kennewick Man and the Paleoamerican World*. Minneapolis: Carolrhoda Books, 2012.

Internet Resources

http://www.washingtonhistory.org/education/families/

Information, educational activities, and online games from the Washington State Historical Society.

http://www.nps.gov/olym/index.htm

The National Park Service's online guide to Olympic National Park.

http://fermi.jhuapl.edu/states/maps1/wa.gif

An excellent relief map of Washington State.

 # Text-Dependent Questions

1. Name the longest river in Washington.
2. Explain the meaning of the slogan "Fifty-four Forty or Fight!"
3. Which fruit does Washington produce more of than any other state?

 # Research Project

The Grand Coulee Dam generates more electricity than any other facility in the United States. Do a brief report on the Grand Coulee. See if you can explain, in simple terms, how it creates electricity.

Index

Numbers in **bold italics** refer to captions.

Series Glossary of Key Terms

bicameral—having two legislative chambers (for example, a senate and a house of representatives).

cede—to yield or give up land, usually through a treaty or other formal agreement.

census—an official population count.

constitution—a written document that embodies the rules of a government.

delegation—a group of persons chosen to represent others.

elevation—height above sea level.

legislature—a lawmaking body.

precipitation—rain and snow.

term limit—a legal restriction on how many consecutive terms an office holder may serve.